Sea Otters

Penguin
Random
House

Series Editor Deborah Lock
US Senior Editor Shannon Beatty
Editor Arpita Nath
Senior Art Editor Ann Cannings
Project Art Editor Tanvi Nathyal
Picture Researcher Sumedha Chopra
Production Editors Christine Ni
Senior Producer, Pre-production Nikoleta Parasaki
DTP Designers Vijay Kandwal, Dheeraj Singh
Jacket Designer Charlotte Jennings
Managing Editor Soma B. Chowdhury
Managing Art Editor Ahlawat Gunjan
Art Director Martin Wilson

Reading Consultant
Linda Gambrell, Ph.D.

First American Edition, 2016
Published in the United States by DK Publishing
345 Hudson Street, New York, New York 10014

Copyright © 2016 Dorling Kindersley Limited
DK, a Division of Penguin Random House LLC
17 18 19 20 10 9 8 7 6 5 4 3
003—285391—June/16

A catalog record for this book is available
from the Library of Congress.
ISBN: 978-1-4654-4456-1 (Paperback)
ISBN: 978-1-4654-4457-8 (Hardback)

DK books are available at special discounts when purchased in bulk for sales promotions, premiums, fund-raising, or educational use. For details, contact:
DK Publishing Special Markets
345 Hudson Street, New York, New York 10014
SpecialSales@dk.com

Printed and bound in U.S.A.

The publisher would like to thank Jim Curland and Frank Reynolds from
Friends of the Sea Otter (www.seaotters.org) for their advice.
The publisher would also like to thank the following for their kind permission to reproduce their photographs:
(Key: a=above, b=below/bottom, c=center, l=left, r=right, t=top)
1 Alamy Images: Harry Walker / Design Pics Inc. 3 iStockphoto.com: RobsonAbbott (br). 4-5 naturepl.com: Bertie Gregory (b). 5 Dreamstime.com: Nilanjan Bhattacharya (cr, br). iStockphoto.com: RobsonAbbott (tc). 6 Getty Images: Stuart Westmorland / The Image Bank (c). 6-7 Getty Images: David Gomez / E+. 8-9 Corbis: Frans Lanting (b). 9 Getty Images: Cameron Rutt / Moment (tl). 10-11 Getty Images: Ai Angel Gentel / Moment Open. 12 123RF.com: Kevin Griffin (bl). 13 naturepl.com: Doc White. 14-15 Getty Images: Jeff Foott. 16 Science Photo Library: Thomas & Pat Leeson (b). 17 Corbis: Hal Beral. 18-19 Corbis: Steven Kazlowski / Science Faction (b). 19 Getty Images: Donald M. Jones / Minden Pictures (tr). 20-21 naturepl.com: Tom Mangelsen. 22 123RF.com: Kevin Griffin (cla). Corbis: Brandon D. Cole (clb); Tim Fitzharris / Minden Pictures (bl). Dreamstime.com: Nilanjan Bhattacharya (tl). 24 Dreamstime.com: Nilanjan Bhattacharya (br) Endpapers: Dreamstime.com: Kristen Wahlquist / Xfkirsten. Jacket credits: Front: Corbis: Kevin Schafer (c). Back: naturepl.com: Bertie Gregory t
All other images © Dorling Kindersley
For further information see: www.dkimages.com

A WORLD OF IDEAS:
SEE ALL THERE IS TO KNOW

www.dk.com

Relaxing

They can float
on their backs.

Grooming

Their fur keeps them
warm and dry.
They brush their fur
and roll over
to keep clean.

whiskers

fur

Swimming

Sea otters use
their webbed feet
and flat tails to swim.

flat tail

webbed foot

Diving

They swim around
to find food.
They dive in and
out of the kelp.   kelp

Eating

They have strong teeth to bite into their food.

crab

teeth

They can hit a stone
on a shellfish to crack
the shell open.

Caring

Otter pups can only float to begin with. Their moms take care of them.

Sleeping

Sea otters may wrap kelp around their bodies when they sleep.

kelp

Glossary

Fur
soft hair covering the skin
of some animals

Kelp
large seaweed
with a long stalk

Shellfish
sea animal
that has a shell

Webbed
fingers or toes joined
with a piece of skin

Whiskers
long hair growing on
the face of some animals

Index

care 18

clean 8

crab 14

dive 12

float 6, 18

food 14

fur 8, 9

kelp 12, 20

pups 18

roll 8

shellfish 16

sleep 20

stone 16

swim 10, 12

tail 10, 11

teeth 14, 15

webbed feet 10, 11

whiskers 8

A Note to Parents

DK Readers is a four-level interactive reading adventure series for children, designed in conjunction with leading literacy experts, including Dr. Linda Gambrell, Distinguished Professor of Education at Clemson University. Dr. Gambrell has served as President of the National Reading Conference, the College Reading Association, and the International Reading Association.

Beautiful illustrations and superb full-color photographs combine with engaging, easy-to-read narratives to offer a fresh approach to each subject in the series. Each DK Reader is guaranteed to capture a child's interest while developing his or her reading skills, general knowledge, and love of reading.

The four levels of DK Readers are aimed at different reading abilities, enabling you to choose the books that are exactly right for your child:

Level 1: Learning to read
Level 2: Beginning to read
Level 3: Beginning to read alone
Level 4: Reading alone

The "normal" age at which a child begins to read can be anywhere from three to eight years old. Adult participation through the lower levels is very helpful for providing encouragement, discussing storylines, and sounding out unfamiliar words.

No matter which level you select, you can be sure that you are helping your child learn to read, then read to learn!

Read about cute and furry sea otters!

Find out all about sea otters as they float, play, and dive for their dinner.

LEARN TO READ, THEN READ TO LEARN!

Engaging stories and fun, interactive pages build reading skills • Developed in consultation with leading literacy experts • Helps build a lifelong love of reading

A level for every reader

  **LEVEL 1 — LEARNING TO READ**

 **LEVEL 2 — BEGINNING TO READ**

 **LEVEL 3 — BEGINNING TO READ ALONE**

LEVEL 4 — READING ALONE

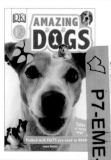

Look out for other great titles!

$3.99 US
$4.99 Canada

ISBN 978-1-4654-4456-1   Printed in U.S.

50399

www.dk.com

P7-EME-458